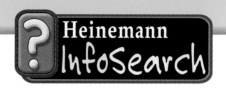

SCIENCE ANSWERS

Electricity

FROM AMPS TO VOLTS

www.heinemann.co.uk/library
Visit our website to find out more information about **Heinemann Library** books.

To order:
 Phone 44 (0) 1865 888066
 Send a fax to 44 (0) 1865 314091
 Visit the Heinemann Bookshop at www.heinemann.co.uk/library to browse our catalogue and order online.

First published in Great Britain by
Heinemann Library, Halley Court,
Jordan Hill, Oxford OX2 8EJ,
part of Harcourt Education.

Heinemann is a registered trademark of
Harcourt Education Ltd.

Editorial: Sarah Eason and Georga Godwin
Design: Jo Hinton-Malivoire and
  Tinstar Design Ltd (www.tinstar.co.uk)
Illustrations: Jeff Edwards
Picture Research: Rosie Garai
  and Liz Eddison
Production: Viv Hichens

Originated by Ambassador Litho Ltd
Printed in Hong Kong, China
 by Wing King Tong

ISBN 0 431 17492 X
08 07 06 05 04
10 9 8 7 6 5 4 3 2 1

**British Library Cataloguing
in Publication Data**
Cooper, Christopher
Electricity. – (Science Answers)
537
A full catalogue record for this book is
available from the British Library.

Acknowledgements
The publishers would like to thank the
following for permission to reproduce
photographs: Corbis/Joseph Sohm **p. 23**;
Corbis/Historical Picture Archive **p. 28**;
Corbis/Jose Luis Pelaez **p. 5**; Digital Stock
p. 4; Liz Eddison **pp. 10, 12, 13, 19**;
Photodisc **p. 15**; Robert Harding **pp. 7, 25**;
Science Photo Library/Cordelia Molloy
p. 22; Science Photo Library/Ferranti
Electronics/A. Sternberg **p. 26**; Science
Photo Library/Novosti Press Agency **p. 17**;
Science Photo Library/Roger Harris **p. 9**;
Tudor Photography **p. 8**.

Cover photograph of the city lights of
Chicago, USA reproduced with permission
of Corbis/Richard Cummins.

The Publishers would like to thank
Robert Snedden and Barbara Katz for
their assistance with the preparation of
this book.

Every effort has been made to contact
copyright holders of any material
reproduced in this book. Any omissions
will be rectified in subsequent printings if
notice is given to the publishers.

Contents

Any words appearing in bold, **like this**, are explained in the Glossary.

About the experiments and demonstrations

In this book you will find sections called 'Science Answers'. This describes an activity that you can try yourself. Here are some safety rules to follow:

- Ask an adult to help with any cutting using a sharp knife.
- Never connect the two terminals of a battery directly together – the large current could burn you.
- Never connect a number of batteries to each other and then connect the last one directly to the first – the large current could burn you.
- Mains electricity is dangerous. Never, ever try to experiment with it.
- Do not experiment with a car battery. This can deliver a dangerous shock.

Materials you will use

Most of these activities can be done with objects that you can find in your own home. A few will need items that you can buy from a hardware shop. You will also need paper and pencil to record your results.

What is electricity?

Our world depends on electricity. Electricity **powers** many of the things we use every day. Machines in our homes are run by electricity – refrigerators, music systems, food-blenders, room heaters and power tools. Machines in offices also use electricity – lifts, air-conditioners, photocopiers and many others. In factories, machines powered by electricity melt metals and lift heavy objects. Other electrical machines drill, stamp and shape materials. At home or at work people are constantly using lights, telephones, computers, radios and TVs – all powered by electricity.

What is electric current?

The electricity that makes a light bulb glow, or a fan turn, is called electric **current**, because it consists of electricity moving (just as a current of water consists of water moving). There are electric currents in nature, too. A stroke of lightning is a powerful but very short-lived electric current.

Making light

Cities blaze with light at night, thanks to electricity. Artificial lighting used to be produced by burning oil or candles. Little work was done after sunset and people went to bed early. When electric lighting became widespread, people continued their daytime activities into the night. Today the centres of large cities are busy 24 hours a day.

How do machines use electricity?

Even when electricity does not provide the actual power that runs a machine, it often helps to make it work. A car engine runs on petrol, but electricity is needed to start the engine. Then, while the engine is running, electricity makes the sparks that make the petrol burn. Electrical instruments send information to the driver about how the engine is working. Many of the driver's controls, such as the indicators and the horn, use electricity.

Pocket power

Mobile phones also need electricity. At the heart of a mobile phone are microchips as complex as those in personal computers. They work by small electric currents, provided by **batteries** that are **portable** stores of electricity.

What is electricity made of?

Electric **current** consists of a stream of **particles**. Various sorts of particle can make electric currents, but the electric current we mainly use is made up of a particular kind of particle called an **electron**. Electrons are parts of **atoms**. All the matter around us is made up of atoms. They are so small that a line of a hundred million atoms would stretch across your fingernail.

Electrons make up the outer layers of each atom and move around a tiny central object called the nucleus (plural *nuclei*) of the atom. The electrons have electric **charge**, which is the scientific name for 'amount of electricity'. The nucleus consists of a different sort of particle, called a **proton**.

How does an electric current flow?

Many sorts of atom can lose electrons easily. Metals are an example. In a metal wire the electrons can easily be made to separate from the atoms and flow through the wire. This stream of electrons is an electric current.

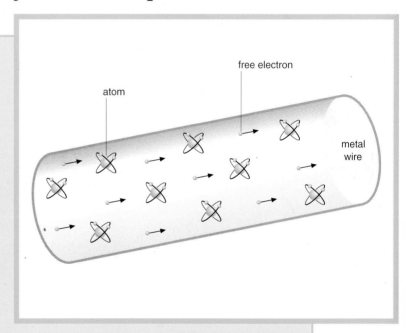

There are wires in **devices** like radios and TVs, and cables (which are just thick wires) carry electricity to our home. They are made of metal – often copper – so that the electrons can move easily.

Is there just one kind of electric charge?

Electrons and protons have different sorts of electric charge. The sort of charge that electrons have is called negative. Protons have a charge called positive. If an object gains electrons, it has a negative charge. If it loses electrons, it has a positive charge because there will then be more protons than electrons in the atoms. Friction is one way that objects can gain or lose electrons. Positive and negative charges attract each other, but all negative charges repel each other (push each other away). All positive charges also repel each other. A short way of saying this is, *'like charges repel, unlike charges attract'*.

Lightning strike

Lightning is electricity in movement. A stream of electrons flows for a fraction of a second from a storm cloud to the ground, or from one cloud to another cloud. The air along the path of the current is heated to about 30,000 °C (about 50,000 °F). This hot air glows and we see the path of the electric current as a bright, zigzagging line – the lightning stroke.

EXPERIMENT: How can we give something an electric charge?

HYPOTHESIS:
Some materials lose or gain electrons when they are rubbed together. This causes an electric charge.

EQUIPMENT:
Balloon and clothing (for example, a sweater).

EXPERIMENT STEPS:
1 Rub a party balloon against a piece of clothing, like a sweater. It will probably stick to the clothing.
2 If this works, put the balloon next to your hair. The balloon attracts your hair too, making the individual strands stand up when the balloon is brought near.
3 Write down what you saw.

CONCLUSION:
The rubbing moves some electrons between the balloon and the sweater. The balloon and sweater each began with exactly equal amounts of positive and negative charge. After rubbing, one has slightly less negative charge and the other has slightly more. These charges are called **static electricity** ('static' means that the charges are at rest). The balloon and the sweater therefore attract each other. (The experiment

can't tell you which way the electrons moved. In fact, electrons tend to move from materials such as wool, cotton or nylon to latex, so in this experiment they almost certainly moved from the clothes to the balloon.)

How can we use static electricity?

A modern photocopying machine uses static electricity. It shines an **image** of, say, a page of a book onto a heated rotating drum that has a positive electric charge on its surface. The light knocks electrons out of atoms under the surface of the drum, and these cancel out some of the positive charge. Where the original page is lighter, the light is brighter, and more electrons are produced. So there is less positive charge on the drum in these parts of the image.

The electrical charge on the drum attracts grains of toner (black powder used in copiers for printing). There is more toner where there is more charge. When the hot drum rolls over a piece of blank paper, it presses toner onto the paper and melts it to form a picture or print that will not rub off.

How can we see Electricity?

Electrons and nuclei in all matter – even our own bodies – push and pull each other all the time. But the total amount of positive charge in any piece of matter is normally exactly equal to the total amount of negative charge. This is because normally there are exactly as many protons as electrons in each atom. (You can see the electrons (blue) and protons (red) in this computer-generated artwork of an atom.) So the total electrical **force** between two objects is normally zero. To show electric effects, we somehow have to separate positive and negative charges from each other.

What happens when you turn on an electric switch?

The electric **current** we use in homes and workplaces comes along cables from giant **power** stations. When the current arrives we need to be able to control it to make it work for us. A switch is one way of doing this. When you flip an electric light switch, you start a current flowing through the bulb. You stop the current by flicking the switch off.

How does the switch work?

The electric current travels along metal wires from the power station. It is easy for current to move through metals. When the switch is on, the current can continue along wires into the lamp or radio, or other device. When you turn the switch off, the switch makes a gap that the current cannot cross. When you turn the switch on again, you close the gap so that the current can flow into the device once more.

Contact!

If you take apart an old torch that isn't needed any more, you may be able to see how the switch works. Switching on brings two pieces of metal together to make a path for the current. Switching off pulls the pieces of metal apart to leave a gap that the current cannot cross.

What materials can current flow through easily?

The wires used in electrical devices are made of metal, because metal has very low resistance making it easier for current to move through it. Low-resistance materials and things made from them are called electrical **conductors**. Wood, rubber and most plastics are examples of electrical **insulators**, which block current. Electrical wires have plastic covers to stop current leaking out. Engineers working on electrical **apparatus** wear plastic-soled shoes to stop currents passing through their bodies to the ground. Electricity can only flow if the **circuit** is complete. Because plastic does not conduct electricity, the plastic soles cause a break in the circuit.

How does a control knob work?

The volume control knob on a radio is an example of another type of control. Turning the knob alters the length of wire that the current flows through. The current is made weaker by having to flow through a longer wire. Scientists and engineers say that the longer wire has a greater **resistance**, because it stops the current from moving so easily.

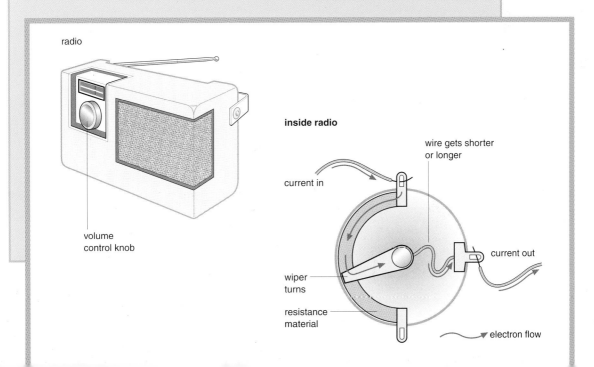

radio

volume
control knob

inside radio

current in

wire gets shorter
or longer

current out

wiper
turns

resistance
material

electron flow

Turn it up!

An electric current works the loudspeaker in a radio. The stronger the current, the louder the sound. The current flows into a coil of wire on its way to the loudspeaker. When the volume control is turned right down, the current is made to go along the whole coil. The resistance of the coil is high, and this makes the current weak. When the control is turned right up, the current goes along only a small part of the coil. This small part of the coil has a small resistance, and so the current is stronger.

How does electricity make things move?

Electric **charges** cause two sorts of **force**. When the charges are **stationary** they cause electrostatic forces ('static' means 'at rest'). After you have rubbed a balloon against your clothes, the balloon and the clothes have stationary charges or **static electricity** on them. The force of attraction between them is electrostatic. The second kind of force is caused by moving charge – electric **current**. These forces are magnetic. Magnetic forces are the sorts of force that affect a compass needle. For example, when there is lightning nearby, a compass needle twitches. It is pulled by the magnetic forces from the powerful current of the lightning stroke. Forces caused by electric current are called electromagnetic.

What is electromagnetism?

Electromagnetic effects are all around us. A compass needle points north–south because of the Earth's magnetism. This magnetism is caused by electric currents in the Earth's core, which consists of hot, molten iron. Every machine or **appliance** that contains an **electric motor**, such as a food mixer or vacuum cleaner, uses electromagnetism generated by an electromagnet, like the one shown here. The electric current going into the **device** is used to generate force, which turns the moving parts.

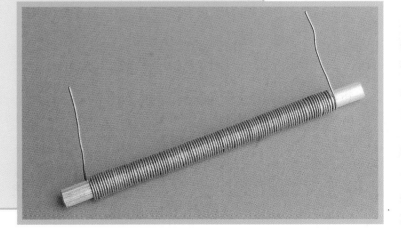

EXPERIMENT: How does electricity make things move?

HYPOTHESIS:
Electric charges can attract or repel other objects, causing them to move.

EQUIPMENT:
Paper, plastic comb, basin with a tap or burette, like in the picture.

EXPERIMENT STEPS:
1 Tear some paper into small pieces.
2 Run a plastic (not metal) comb through your hair several times quickly.
3 Then hold the comb close to the pieces of paper. You'll see the pieces jump up and stick to the comb. If they don't, try a comb made of another kind of plastic.
4 Now run water from a tap. Have the tap only slightly open, so that the water is a slow, thin stream. Run the comb through your hair again and hold it near the top of the stream of water.

5 Write down what you saw.

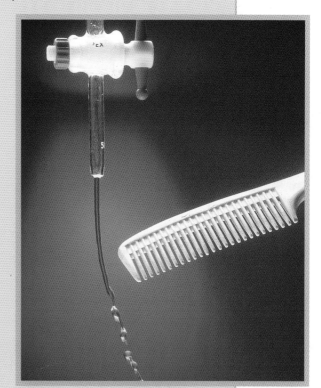

CONCLUSION:
After you have combed, there are **electrons** on the plastic that have been removed from your hair. They attract the water and the paper in the same way that balloons rubbed against clothes attract the clothes. This is an electrostatic force.

What are amps, ohms and volts?

Scientists measure the amount of electricity in units called **coulombs** (symbol C). One coulomb is the amount of charge on about 6 billion billion electrons.

Electric **current** is described in amps (symbol A). A current of 1 amp is 1 coulomb of charge flowing every second. Electric current needs a 'push' to make it flow. The amount of push is measured in units called volts (symbol V), and it is usually called **voltage**. How much current flows depends on the voltage pushing it and on the resistance of the **circuit** that it flows through. The unit of **resistance** is the ohm (symbol Ω, a Greek letter pronounced 'omega').

Just about the size of it

Here are some facts about typical household electric appliances:

Current used
Typical electric kettle: 4 amps
Typical light bulb: 0.4 amp
Pocket calculator: 0.07 amp

Voltage
AA-size **batteries**: 1.5 volts
Electric mains: in the United Kingdom and Australia, about 230 volts (in many countries about 110 volts).

Resistance
Typical kettle: about 58 ohms (in the UK)
Ordinary light bulb: about 600 ohms

The right voltage for the job

Electric current is carried from electricity generating stations across country along metal wires slung from towers called **pylons**. This current is at several hundred thousand volts, because this is best for sending currents long distances.

It would be dangerous to use very high voltages in factories, offices or the home. So the cross-country cables lead to **substations**, where machines called **transformers** automatically reduce the voltage. Some cables then take electricity to factories, while others take a still lower-voltage supply to homes.

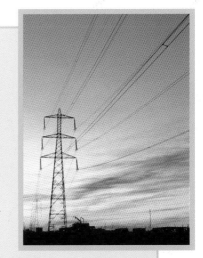

How does a generator produce electricity?

An electric current produces its own magnetism, but the reverse also happens. If magnetism passes through an electric **circuit** and the magnetism varies in strength or direction, a **voltage** is produced in the circuit. If the magnetism does not change, but the circuit moves, a voltage is also produced in the circuit.

What happens in a power station **generator** is more complicated. The stationary part of the generator is an **electromagnet**, and its magnetic field passes through the coils of the rotor. When the coils spin, a voltage is produced in the rotor. The spinning motion generates electricity at about 25,000 volts.

In a very simple generator, an electric current can be produced just by rotating a coil of wire between the poles (ends) of a magnet.

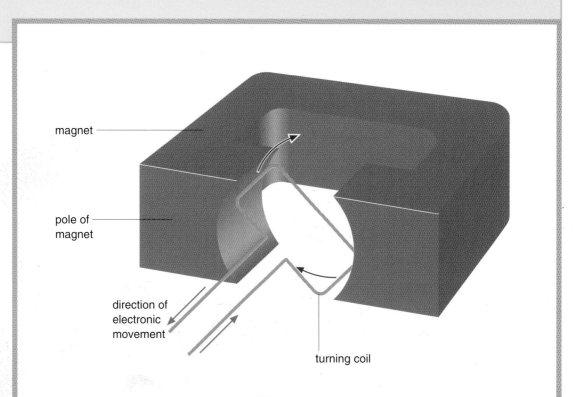

magnet

pole of magnet

direction of electronic movement

turning coil

Electricity for homes, offices and factories is produced by generators in power stations. In most power stations the rotor is turned by steam. The steam is produced by heating water by burning fossil fuels such as oil, gas and coal. Nuclear **energy** can also be used. Hydroelectric power stations use the power of falling water. Electricity can also be generated by solar panels, which convert the energy of sunlight into electricity.

Two-way current

The **current** produced by a spinning generator in a power station isn't a steady one-way current. It goes first in one direction in the wire, then in the other. It is called **alternating current (AC)**. ('Alternating' means 'reversing'.) Many sorts of machine, such as drills and food mixers, work better on AC than **DC (direct current)**. Very importantly, **transformers** need AC to work with.

'Wet' electricity

A very common way of running electricity generators is **hydroelectric energy**. This is the power provided by waterfalls or water flowing out of reservoirs (artificial lakes made by dams). This form of electricity generation has long been used in mountainous areas such as Norway.

What other ways of generating electricity do we have?

Electricity can be generated by wind power. A wind turbine is a giant fan turned by the wind. 'Wind farms' consisting of dozens or hundreds of them have been built in a few windy places. A very large wind farm can produce as much electricity as an ordinary power station.

Ocean waves have also been harnessed to generate electricity. One type of wave-power device is a 'duck'. This is a floating hollow canister, tethered to the seabed. About 25 of them are linked together in a chain. They rock as waves pass, and the turning motion is harnessed to turn an electricity generator. The electricity is sent to the shore along a cable. Hundreds of chains of 'ducks' working together can produce a useful amount of electricity.

Solar energy

Another source of energy for electricity generation is the energy of sunlight, or solar energy. Very large **installations** have been built in which hundreds of large mirrors reflect sunlight onto a boiler, raising its temperature enough to boil the water. The steam then drives a generator in the usual way.

Photoelectric cells

More commonly, smaller power units are used in which **photoelectric cells** generate electricity directly from the energy of sunlight. When sunlight falls on photoelectric cells, they produce a weak voltage. Solar energy is used to generate electricity in pocket calculators, on spacecraft and in remote scientific research stations.

Scientists' fears

Many people argue that we should reduce the amount of gas, oil, coal and uranium that we use. They think we will run out of oil quite soon and the carbon dioxide produced by burning oil and coal will cause our atmosphere to trap more of the Sun's energy, which we call global warming. This would raise the temperature of the Earth. There are also fears that nuclear energy produces dangerous and long-lasting radioactive waste.

DEMONSTRATION: Light on the problem.

If you have a solar-powered calculator, you can see the effect of altering the amount of light that falls on it.

DEMONSTRATION STEPS:

1 Turn the calculator on. See what happens to the display if you shade the photoelectric cells. (These are visible as a dark panel on the top of the calculator.)

2 See what happens when you shine a bright light onto the cells (but don't make the calculator or the photoelectric cells hot by bringing a lamp too close).

3 Write down what you saw.

CONCLUSION:

The photoelectric cells stop working when light stops shining on them, or soon afterwards. They work more strongly when the light is brighter.

How do batteries work?

Batteries are handy and **portable** stores of electricity. Chemical reactions inside them generate electricity. Each battery has two terminals, or metal contacts. In some types of battery, there are two studs at the top. In others, two metal strips stick out at the top. In the case of the small 'button batteries' used in watches and calculators, the top and bottom of the metal case are the two contacts.

When an external **circuit** is connected to the battery's terminals, the chemical reactions begin.

These reactions cause **electrons** to flow from one terminal to the other inside the battery. The stream of electrons then continues out of the battery. The electrons flow along conducting materials, such as copper wires, through a device such as a lamp or a radio. They then flow back into the battery.

What should we call batteries?

The correct name for most of the batteries we use is 'cell'. The word 'battery' should strictly only be applied to several cells joined together. A 1.5-volt battery is actually a cell. A 9-volt battery consists of six 1.5-volt cells joined together. A car battery typically consists of six 2-volt cells.

How are batteries constructed?

Every cell has two **electrodes**, made of different materials. In one type of AA battery, one electrode is the zinc case of the cell. The other electrode is a carbon rod inside, connected to a metal cap on the cell. In every cell there is a special material between the two electrodes, called the electrolyte. In a torch battery this material is a paste containing chemicals. In a car battery it is a liquid – dilute sulphuric acid.

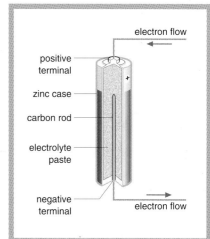

electron flow

positive terminal

zinc case

carbon rod

electrolyte paste

negative terminal

electron flow

EXPERIMENT: How can I make a simple battery?

HYPOTHESIS:
You can make a battery by dipping two different metals into acid. Follow the steps below to find out how this works.

EQUIPMENT:
Four small pieces of copper, 4 small pieces of zinc, 4 potatoes, 5 pieces of electrical wire, 8 crocodile clips, torch bulb in a bulb-holder. If you cannot find strips of metal, you can try large screws or nails of different metals.

EXPERIMENT STEPS:

1 Stick the pieces of metal into a potato and attach the wires as shown.
2 Touch the other ends of the wires to your tongue. The tingle and strange taste are caused by a weak electric **current** from your battery!
3 Now connect four of the potatoes in series as shown in the diagram. You should be able to get enough **voltage** from them to make the torch bulb glow.
4 Write down what you saw.

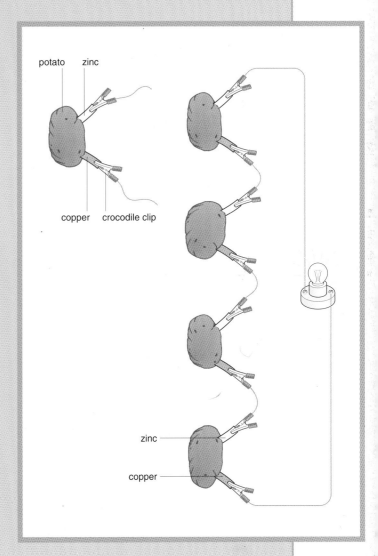

CONCLUSION:
Dipping two different metals into acid can make a battery – and potatoes have enough acid inside them to make a battery.

How do we use electricity?

One way in which electricity is useful is in making heat and light. An electric light bulb contains a wire made of a metal such as tungsten. The wire is heated by the **current** passing through it and glows white-hot.

The wire gets hot because the electrons moving in the current bump against the **atoms** of the metal, making the atoms vibrate faster. Heat just *is* the vibration of atoms.

The more the electrons bump against the atoms, the harder it is for the current to flow – that is, the higher the **resistance** of the wire. So a high-resistance wire produces more heat.

Warmth from electricity

But electrical heat can also be used for itself, not just as a means of making light. In an oven the current is used to heat coils of wire built into the hotplates. Heat passes from the coils into the hotplates.

The same principle is used in room heaters, irons and electric kettles. In a hairdryer coils of wire are heated. The same current is used to drive a fan, which blows a stream of air over the hot coils.

Electricity making movement

An **electric motor** is like an electric **generator** in reverse. In the generator, rotation causes electric current to flow. In the motor, electric current causes rotation. In the motor there is a **rotor**, consisting of a set of coils that act as **electromagnets** when current flows. Surrounding the rotor there is either a set of magnets or an armature, consisting of coils of wire that also act as electromagnets when current flows. The magnetic forces make the rotor turn.

Motors like this turn household fans and hairdryers. In a car an electric motor is used to start the petrol engine. Smaller electric motors open and close powered windows in some cars. Many trains are driven by electric motors. The electricity may be supplied from a **power** rail or overhead power lines. Or it may be produced by a diesel engine in the locomotive. Some cars also use electric motors. They need to recharge their batteries at refueling stations like the one shown here.

How do we turn sound into electricity?

Sound reproduction depends on the production of an electric current with a strength that is **variable** from moment to moment in the same way that the loudness of the sound is variable.

A very simple sort of microphone is used in telephones. The sound of the user's voice makes a metal plate in the telephone's microphone vibrate. The plate presses against carbon in the form of tiny grains, alternately harder, reducing the resistance, and more gently, increasing the resistance. A small electric current passes through the carbon constantly. As the resistance changes, the current changes in strength.

How is electricity turned back into sound?

When the current from a telephone microphone is passed into a telephone loudspeaker, it goes through a coil, which behaves as an electromagnet. The coil attracts a magnet attached to a cone-shaped piece of metal or other material. The rapidly varying current causes the strength of the magnetism to change rapidly. This in turn causes the cone to vibrate.

The vibrating cone sets up vibrations in the air. These vibrations are sounds (because a sound is simply a vibration in the air). The sounds are a copy of the sounds that struck the microphone.

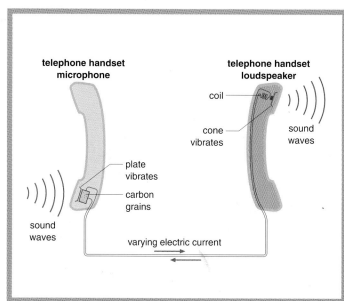

How does electricity make pictures?

The lens on the front of a TV camera forms an **image** inside the camera. The electronics inside the camera 'read' this image from side to side and from top to bottom, 30 times per second (in the UK).

Inside the TV receiver tube, beams of **electrons** sweep from side to side and top to bottom, 'painting' the picture on the inside of the screen. The electrons strike dots of materials that then glow. The stronger the beam (that is, the more electrons in it), the brighter the material glows.

What are microchips?

At the heart of almost every electronic **device** today is a microchip. This is a small piece of **semiconductor** material. Semiconductors let current pass, but less easily than a **conductor** does. The elements silicon and germanium are examples. Semiconductors have special properties that make them valuable for building electrical **circuits**.

A microchip is typically about 6 mm square. On its surface is a circuit made by adding small quantities of other materials in the pattern of the circuit. The circuit can contain millions of electronic components.

How do computers use microchips?

Inside a personal computer, a small number of microchips work together. One is the CPU, or central processing unit. This is the 'brain' of the PC. Other chips control the monitor display, the sound and other functions. Each microchip is packaged in a plastic container, with metal pins sticking out. The pins make contact with the PCB, or printed circuit board. This is a board carrying a circuit of copper pathways, which are literally printed on a flat surface. Microchips and other **components** can be plugged in at various points around the board. There is even a fan to cool the inside of the computer.

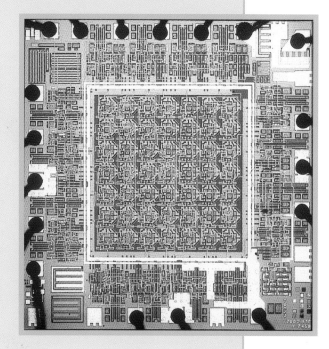

EXPERIMENT: How does the electricity supplied affect how a motor runs?

HYPOTHESIS:

A motor can be driven by electricity. Other components connected in series mean that less power reaches the motor.

EQUIPMENT:

Small electric motor, 2 flat 4.5 V **batteries**, several lengths of wire, 1 bulb and bulb-holder.

EXPERIMENT STEPS:

1 You may find an electric motor inside a battery-powered toy car, or inside a hand-held fan. Ask an adult to help you remove it.
2 Then test the motor using batteries and the set-up shown in the diagram.
3 Touch the wires from the battery terminals to the motor's contacts, and see the engine turn.
4 Try the effect of putting extra resistance in the circuit – for example, a torch bulb.
5 Write down what you saw.

CONCLUSION:

When components are connected in series, each one receives less electricity. If another battery is added, the supply of electricity to the circuit increases.

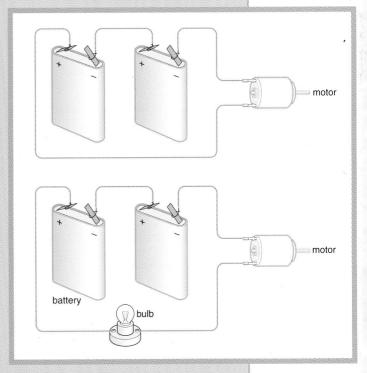

People who found the answers

André Marie Ampère (1775–1836)

The French scientist André Marie Ampère was one of the first scientists to make it clear that electricity and magnetism are closely connected. He discovered how the strength of an electric **current's magnetic field** is related to the strength of the current and the length of the **conductor** through which it flows. And he discovered how two wires carrying electric currents attract each other or push each other apart, depending on the direction of the currents.

Michael Faraday (1791–1867)

Faraday studied how electric currents make chemical reactions happen. He also found that changing a magnetic field can make an electric current flow – the basis of modern electricity generation.

Faraday found it much easier to think in pictures than in mathematical symbols. He invented the way of showing magnetic fields as lines of force that is widely used today.

Amazing facts

- Some fish use electricity as a weapon. The torpedo fish can grow up to 1.8 m (6 ft) long and can deliver an electric current repeatedly into the surrounding water. Small fish nearby are stunned, and the torpedo fish can easily catch and eat them. The electric eel, which grows up to 3 m (10 ft) long, can do the same. Some fish produce weaker electric currents, which they use to send signals to each other, or to detect obstacles in the water.

- The battery was invented by an Italian scientist who was so fascinated by electricity that he even wrote a poem about electricity in Latin. Alessandro Volta experimented with different metals to try to make an electric current, and by 1800 had succeeded. His first battery used curved bars of copper and zinc dipping into bowls of salty water. Later Volta improved the design by stacking up discs of copper, zinc and cardboard soaked in salty water. A current would flow when the top and bottom of this 'Voltaic pile' were connected.

- It's often said that 'lightning doesn't strike in the same place twice' – but that's very wrong! The tallest tree or building in an area is likely to be struck whenever there's a thunderstorm. The tallest skyscrapers may be struck hundreds of times in a year. However, tall buildings are fitted with lightning conductors – strips of metal running from the top of the building into the ground. The electricity of the lightning stroke usually flows harmlessly along this.

- In the mid-18th century, Benjamin Franklin, scientist and Founding Father of the United States, entertained dinner guests with a turkey that he tried to kill with electric shock, and cooked before a fire lit by an electric spark. Franklin also gave them glasses previously charged with static electricity and enjoyed their reactions as they received mild shocks.

Glossary

alternating current (AC) electric current that flows first one way and then the other

apparatus equipment used for a particular purpose

appliance another word for device. Often used when talking about machinery in the home.

atom smallest piece of a chemical element that can exist on its own. It consists of smaller, electrically charged particles, including electrons and protons.

battery device that generates electric current by a chemical reaction

charge amount of electricity. Charge can be of two kinds, called positive and negative.

circuit arrangement of electrical components through which current can flow to do some job

component part of something larger, usually a machine

conductor material or object that electric current can flow through

coulomb unit of electric charge. It is equal to the charge carried by 6.28 billion billion electrons.

current flow of electric charge.

device something made for a special purpose. Sometimes called a gadget.

direct current (DC) electric current that flows in one direction all the time

electric field pattern of electrical influence produced by an electric charge or a changing magnetic field

electric motor machine that converts electrical energy into motion

electrode conductor through which electrons enter and leave an electrical device

electromagnet device that develops a magnetic field when electric current is passed through it

electron negatively charged particle found in every atom. Most electric current is a flow of electrons and protons.

energy measure of a system's ability to make things happen: move objects, generate heat or light, make chemical reactions occur and so on

force influence that alters or moves an object

generator machine for producing an electric current. It is usually driven by steam.

hydroelectric energy electrical energy generated by a river or a stream of water from a lake or reservoir

image picture of something

installation something that is placed somewhere for a particular purpose

insulator material or object that electric current cannot easily flow through

magnetic field pattern of magnetic influence produced by a magnet or by electric current

photoelectric cell device that generates electricity when light strikes it

particle tiny piece of matter

portable able to be carried around easily

power 1) rate at which energy transferred from one place to another 2) energy put to work, for example, 'nuclear power', 'electrical power' and 'steam power'

proton positively charged particle found in every atom. Most electric current is a flow of protons and electrons.

pylon tall mast that carries electricity cables

quantity measured amount of something

resistance measure of how easily electric current passes through something

rotor rotating coil in an electric motor or generator

semiconductor material with a resistance between that of an insulator and a conductor. Microchips are made from semiconductors.

static electricity non-moving electric charge on an object, due to its losing or gaining electrons

stationary not moving

substation place where the voltage of the electricity supply is reduced for use in factories, offices and homes

transformer device for altering the voltage of alternating current

variable not always the same. Capable of changing.

voltage 'push' that makes electric current flow. Voltage is produced by chemical reactions, magnetism or other means.

Index

More books to read

Science Fact Files: Electricity and Magnetism, Steve Parker
    (Hodder Wayland, 2001)
Science in Our World: Electricity and Magnetism, Brian J Knapp
    (Atlantic Europe Publishing Co Ltd, 1991)
Science Topics: Electricity and Magnetism, Anne Fullick and
    Chris Oxlade (Heinemann Library, 2000)
Focus on Science: Electricity, Barbara Taylor
    (Franklin Watts, 2003)